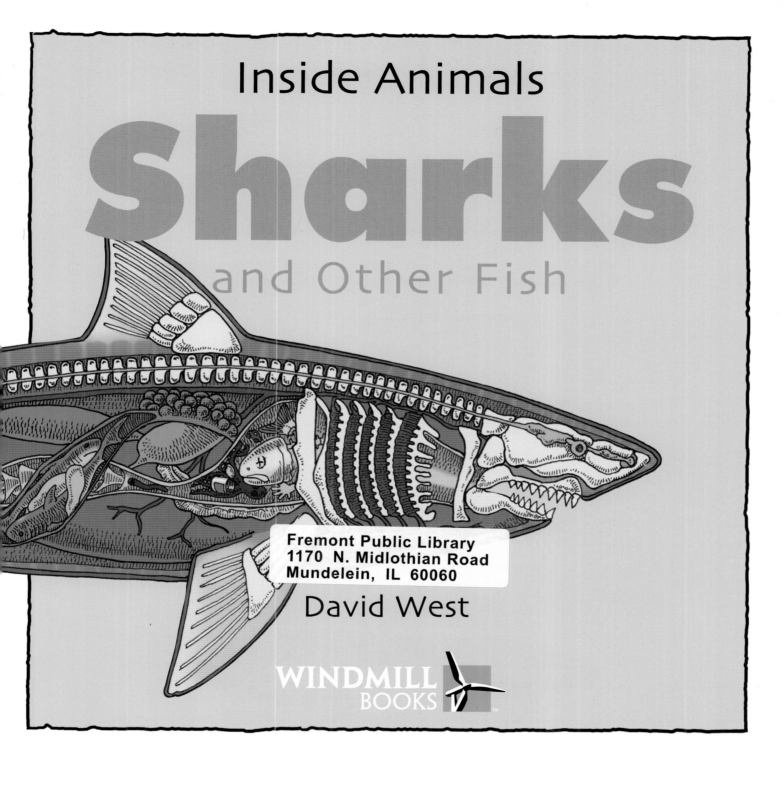

Inside Animals
Sharks
and Other Fish

David West

WINDMILL
BOOKS

Published in 2018 by **Windmill Books**,
an imprint of Rosen Publishing
29 East 21st Street, New York, NY 10010

Designed and illustrated *by* David West

CATALOGING-IN-PUBLICATION DATA
Names: West, David.
Title: Sharks and other fish / David West.
Description: New York : Windmill Books, 2018. | Series: Inside animals | Includes index.
Identifiers: ISBN 9781508194293 (pbk.) | ISBN 9781508193913 (library bound) |
ISBN 9781508194354 (6 pack)
Subjects: LCSH: Sharks–Juvenile literature. | Fishes–Juvenile literature.
Classification: LCC QL617.2 W47 2018 | DDC 597'.03–dc23

Manufactured in China

CPSIA Compliance Information: Batch BW18WM: For Further Information contact Rosen Publishing, New York, New York at 1-800-237-9932

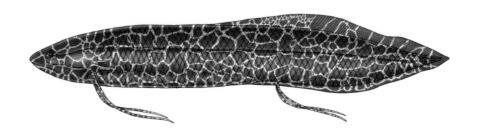

Contents

Ray-finned fish

Most fish are ray-finned fish. They are called this because their fins are made of skin stretched over a ray of bones. They are members of the family of fish that has a bony skeleton. Most ray-finned fish are covered in **scales**. They are cold-blooded, and the females lay eggs.

Ray-finned fish can be found in the sea and in fresh water. This carp lives in freshwater lakes and rivers. They feed on plants, insects, and **crustaceans** on the river or lake bed.

Inside a Ray-finned fish

Tail
Like most fish, it uses its tail to power itself forward as it wriggles through the water.

Dorsal fin
This fin on the back helps keep the fish from rolling as it swims along.

Spine

Skeleton
The muscled body of ray-finned fish is supported by a skeleton of skull, spine, and fine bones.

Bladder

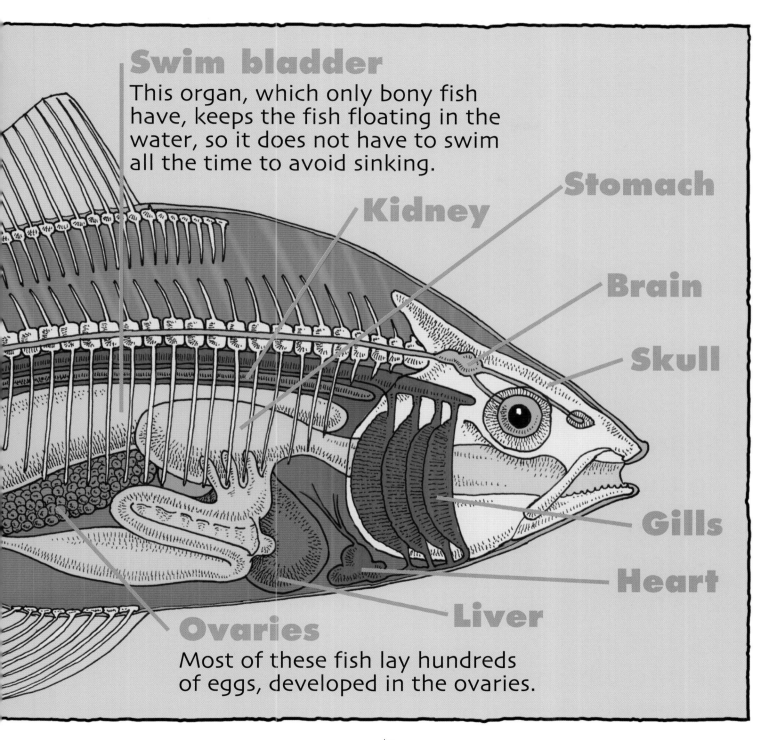

Swim bladder

This organ, which only bony fish have, keeps the fish floating in the water, so it does not have to swim all the time to avoid sinking.

Kidney

Stomach

Brain

Skull

Gills

Heart

Liver

Ovaries

Most of these fish lay hundreds of eggs, developed in the ovaries.

Shark

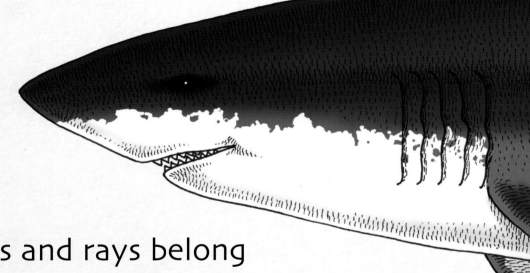

Sharks and rays belong
to the family of fish that do not
have a bony skeleton. Instead their
skeleton is made of **cartilage**. Shark scales
are not like the scales of bony fish. Their
bodies are covered in tiny, sharp, v-shaped
scales, which are rough to the touch.

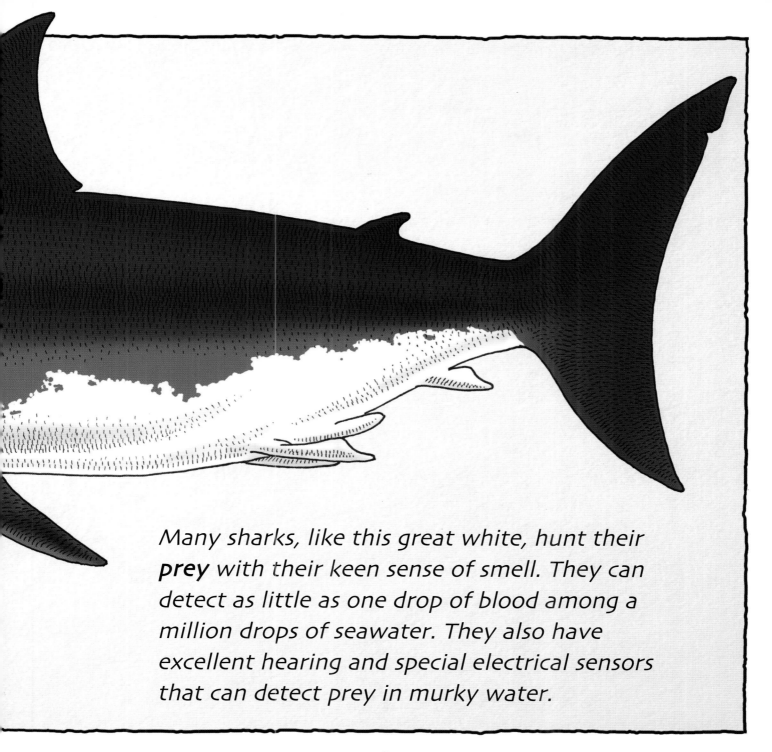

Many sharks, like this great white, hunt their **prey** with their keen sense of smell. They can detect as little as one drop of blood among a million drops of seawater. They also have excellent hearing and special electrical sensors that can detect prey in murky water.

Inside a **Shark**

Nose
A shark can detect a single drop of blood in a million drops of water.

Skin
The skin's surface is made of tiny scales called denticles. It feels like sandpaper.

Ovary

Brain

Teeth
Most sharks have five rows of teeth. When a tooth falls out, it is replaced by the one behind.

Gills
Gills work like lungs. They extract oxygen from the water and transfer it to the blood that is pumped through them.

Heart

Stomach

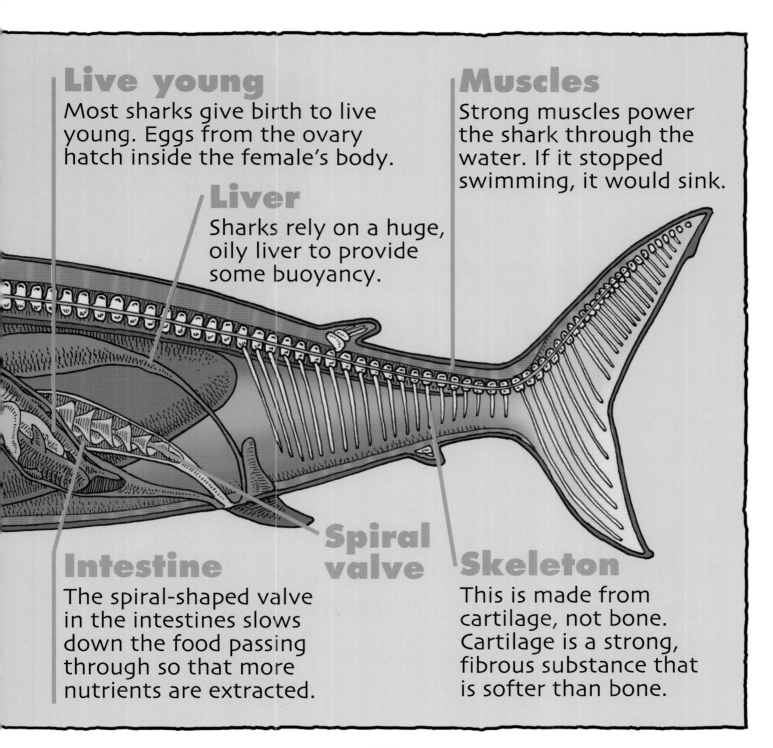

Live young

Most sharks give birth to live young. Eggs from the ovary hatch inside the female's body.

Muscles

Strong muscles power the shark through the water. If it stopped swimming, it would sink.

Liver

Sharks rely on a huge, oily liver to provide some buoyancy.

Intestine

The spiral-shaped valve in the intestines slows down the food passing through so that more nutrients are extracted.

Spiral valve

Skeleton

This is made from cartilage, not bone. Cartilage is a strong, fibrous substance that is softer than bone.

Seahorse

Seahorses are fish that swim upright. They have a swim bladder and breathe through gills. They don't have scales. Their skin is stretched over an outside skeleton called an exoskeleton. They have long tails which they use to grasp weeds or coral. They are good at camouflaging themselves to avoid **predators**. They can change color very quickly to match their surroundings.

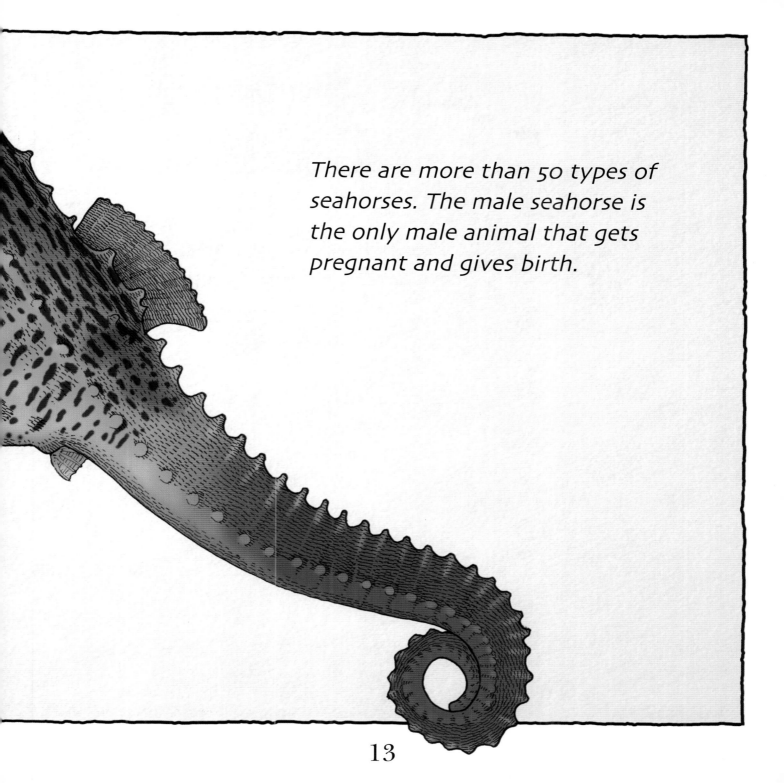

There are more than 50 types of seahorses. The male seahorse is the only male animal that gets pregnant and gives birth.

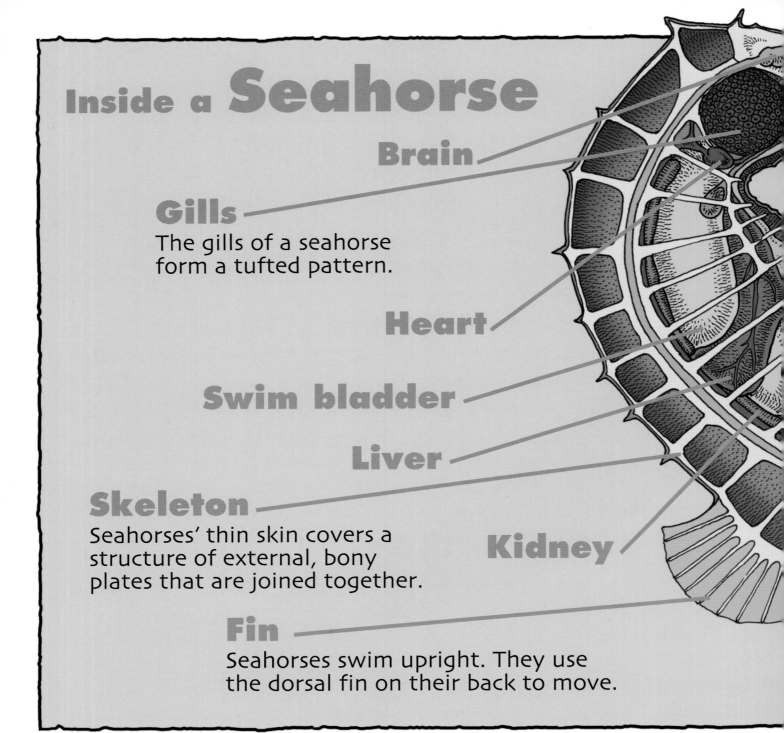

Inside a Seahorse

Brain

Gills

The gills of a seahorse form a tufted pattern.

Heart

Swim bladder

Liver

Skeleton

Seahorses' thin skin covers a structure of external, bony plates that are joined together.

Kidney

Fin

Seahorses swim upright. They use the dorsal fin on their back to move.

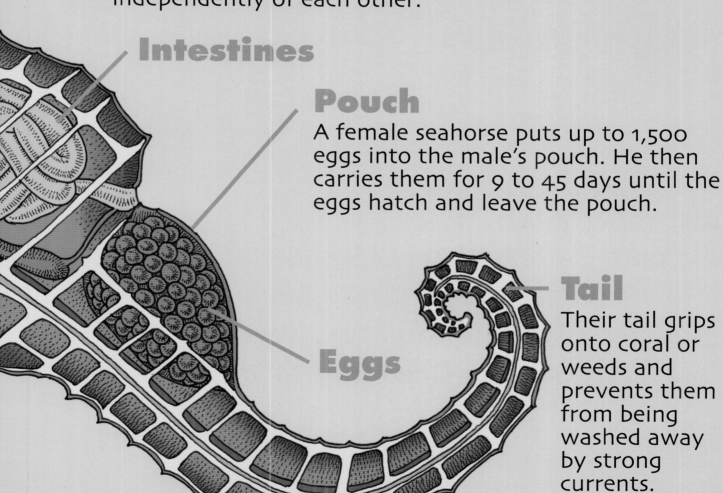

Snout
Seahorses use their long snouts to suck up food like a vacuum cleaner.

Eyes
Seahorses' eyes move independently of each other.

Intestines

Pouch
A female seahorse puts up to 1,500 eggs into the male's pouch. He then carries them for 9 to 45 days until the eggs hatch and leave the pouch.

Eggs

Tail
Their tail grips onto coral or weeds and prevents them from being washed away by strong currents.

Lamprey

Lampreys are long, eel-like, jawless fish. They have large eyes. Their head has one nostril on the top and seven gill openings on each side. They have a funnel-like, sucking mouth with teeth. Some feed by latching onto their prey and sucking their blood.

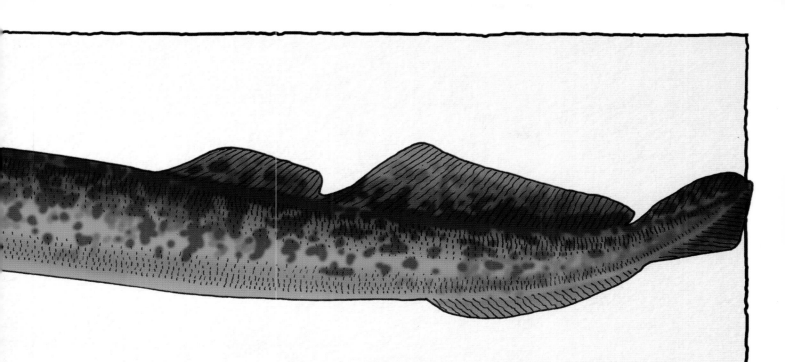

Most lampreys live in coastal waters and freshwater. However, some lampreys, such as this sea lamprey, live mainly in the ocean. Sea lampreys are born in rivers and travel downstream to the sea. They return to the river to **spawn** before dying.

Inside a **Lamprey**

Nostril

Lampreys have a good sense of smell. They have only one nostril which is located on top of their head.

Brain

Heart

Liver

Kidney

Sucking mouth

Lampreys feed on prey by attaching their mouths to a fish's body. Their teeth cut through the skin and scales until they reach blood and body fluid.

Gills

Instead of water entering the mouth, it is pumped in and out of the seven gill holes on each side of the head.

18

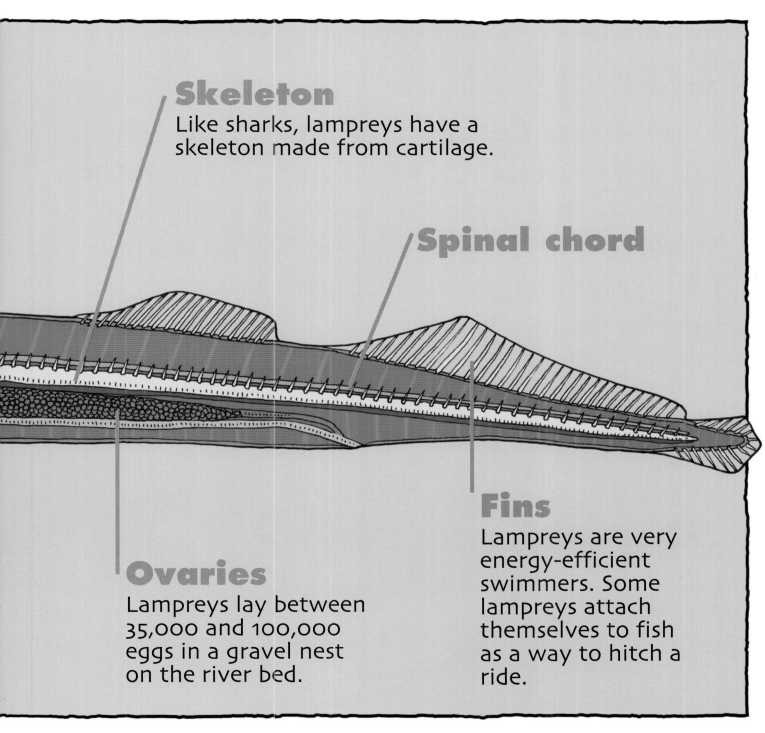

Skeleton
Like sharks, lampreys have a skeleton made from cartilage.

Spinal chord

Ovaries
Lampreys lay between 35,000 and 100,000 eggs in a gravel nest on the river bed.

Fins
Lampreys are very energy-efficient swimmers. Some lampreys attach themselves to fish as a way to hitch a ride.

Lungfish

Lungfish are freshwater fish that feed on fish, insects, crustaceans, and plants. They are the only fish that can breathe air both out of water, using lungs, and underwater, using gills. Some lungfish can survive droughts by burrowing into mud and hibernating until the rains return.

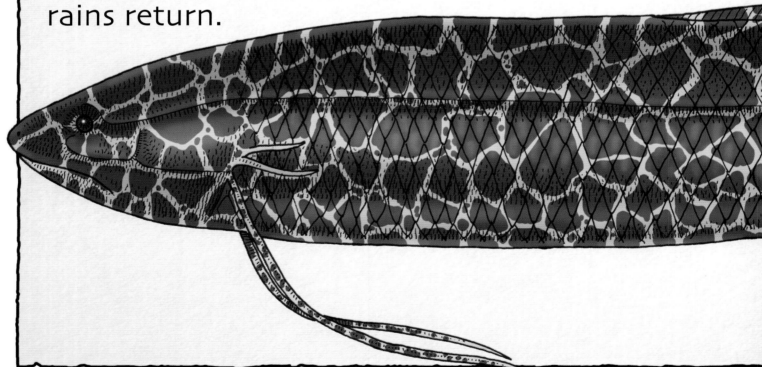

Lungfish like this marbled lungfish live in swamps, river beds, flood plains, and river deltas in Africa. After the females spawn, males guard the nest of eggs from attack for about eight weeks.

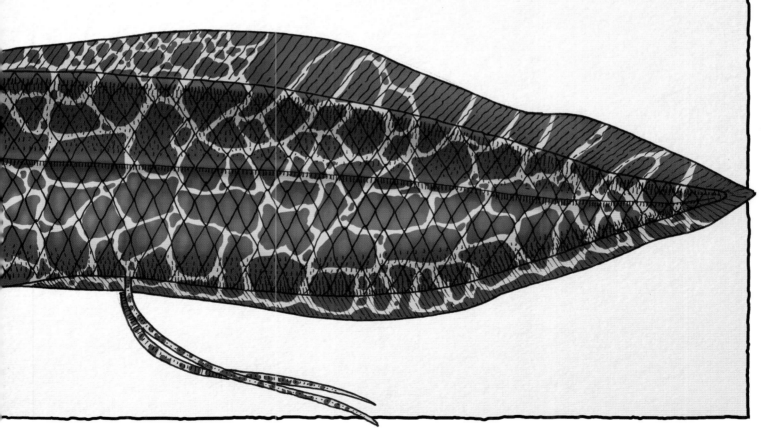

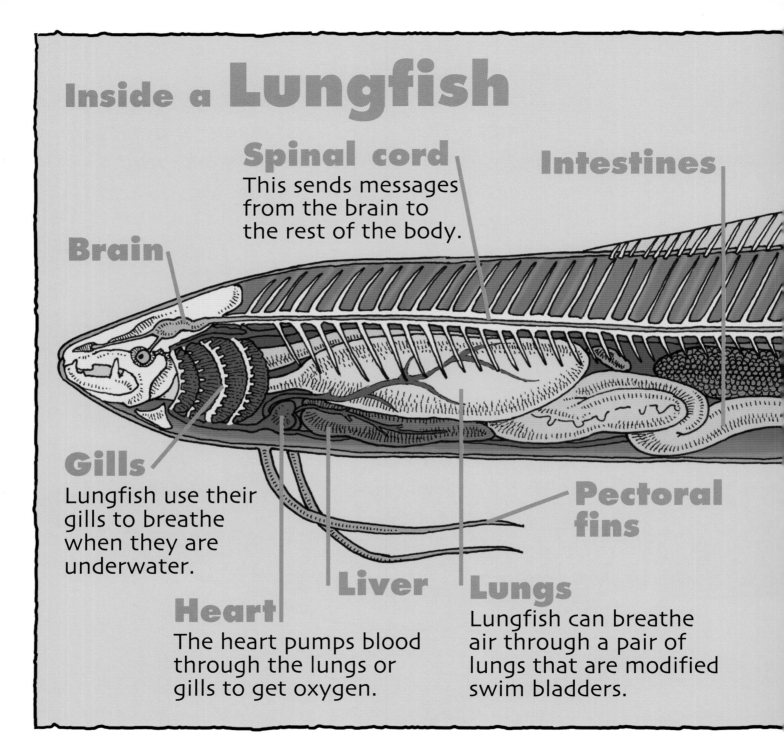

Inside a Lungfish

Spinal cord
This sends messages from the brain to the rest of the body.

Intestines

Brain

Gills
Lungfish use their gills to breathe when they are underwater.

Pectoral fins

Liver

Heart
The heart pumps blood through the lungs or gills to get oxygen.

Lungs
Lungfish can breathe air through a pair of lungs that are modified swim bladders.

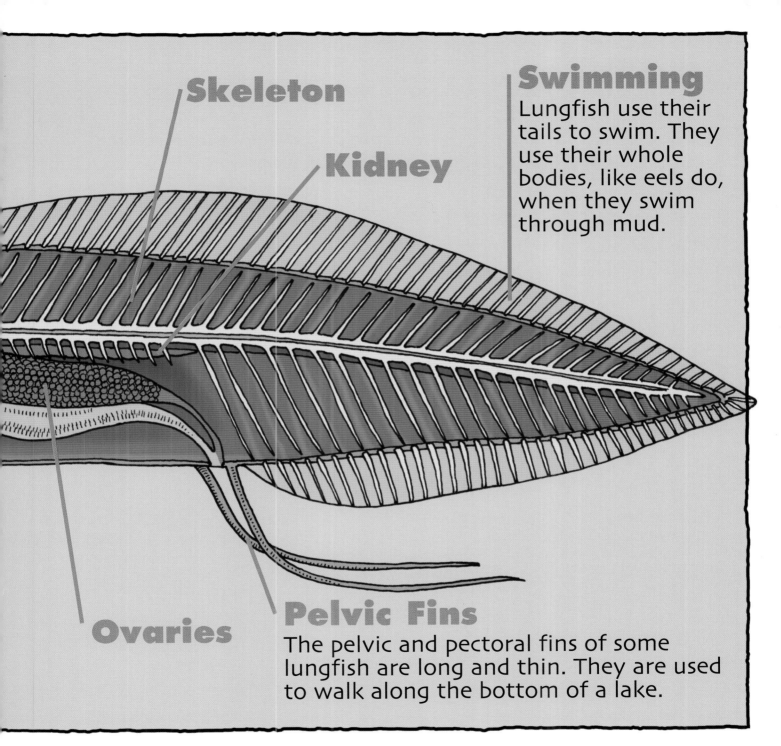

Skeleton

Kidney

Swimming
Lungfish use their tails to swim. They use their whole bodies, like eels do, when they swim through mud.

Ovaries

Pelvic Fins
The pelvic and pectoral fins of some lungfish are long and thin. They are used to walk along the bottom of a lake.

Glossary

cartilage A strong, fibrous substance that is softer than bone.

crustacean A group of mainly water animals that includes crabs, lobsters, and shrimps.

predator An animal that hunts and eats other animals.

prey An animal that is hunted and eaten by another animal.

scales Thin bony plates that cover and protect the skin of a fish or reptile.

spawn The release or laying of eggs by a fish or amphibian.

Index